# contents

# THE HISTORY OF DEBATE

**IN ANCIENT GREECE,** THE ATHENIANS USED THE ART OF **PUBLIC SPEAKING** TO DEBATE IMPORTANT ISSUES OF ETHICS **AND** MORALITY.

*On the issue of* **truth...**

> So little trouble do men take in the search after truth that they prefer to accept whatever comes first to hand...

> I see no wrong in putting more reliance on the exaggerated embellishments of the storyteller to please the ear...

WHEN **DEMOCRACY** CRUMBLED, PUBLIC DEBATES BECAME A VERY DANGEROUS FORM OF **COMMUNICATION.**

# SOCRATES,

THE GREAT GREEK PHILOSOPHER, WAS SENTENCED TO DEATH BECAUSE THE NEW POWER HOLDERS IN ATHENS **DISAGREED** WITH HIM!

Socrates, we disagree with what you say. Therefore, you will be put to death!

?

# TODAY,

IN MOST SOCIETIES, DEBATERS EXPLORE **DIFFERING OPINIONS** WITHOUT RISK TO LIFE.

**THE ISSUES** EXPLORED IN THIS BOOK MAY BE DIFFERENT FROM THOSE DEBATED BY THE ANCIENT GREEKS, BUT EXPLORING THE **SUPPORTING ARGUMENTS** AND REBUTTALS FOR SUCH ISSUES CAN STILL INFLUENCE AND CHANGE THE WAY WE SEE THINGS.

# SAVE THE PLANET: ~~STOP~~ EATING MEAT

**CLARIFY**

vegetarian
erode
sequestered
filtration
steroids
obesity

**WOULD YOU** be a vegetarian if it gave starving people the **chance to eat**? In today's world, there is no excuse for eating meat. **Global overpopulation** demands that we stop feeding nearly a half of the world's grain harvest to hard-hoofed animals, such as cattle, pigs and sheep, that erode the soil and contribute to global warming. Instead, we should plant **vegetable crops** that can feed many more people.

**OPINION**

What is your stance on this issue? Why?

## PRODUCING MEAT IS A HUGE AND UNNECESSARY WASTE OF RESOURCES.

Four hectares of farming land can support 60 people with a **soya bean crop**, 24 people with **wheat**, 10 people with **corn** and only two people with **cattle**. It takes one calorie of fossil fuel to produce a calorie of plant food, as opposed to 78 calories of fossil fuel to produce one calorie of beef protein. The **Amazon rainforest** – a vital source of sequestered carbon, air filtration and botanical medicines, as well as a home for its indigenous people – is being cut down **even as you read this** to graze cows that **WILL BECOME HAMBURGERS.**

### Literary Tool

**Rhetorial Question** – a question that does not require an answer. Find any?

**ANYONE WHO HAS EVER HAD A PET KNOWS THAT ANIMALS HAVE FEELINGS.** They can be happy, sad, excited, frightened – **just like people**. Imagine eating your pet! What is the difference between this animal's feelings and those of other animals? Many animals that are slaughtered for meat are raised in **horrific factory conditions**. They are imprisoned in tiny cages, miserable and often in pain, and pumped full of **antibiotics**, **hormones**, **steroids** and other drugs. These chemicals are stored in the animals' bodies and then absorbed by people eating meat.

As well as **caring about animals**, we should be vegetarian for our own **health**. Our molar teeth are designed for grinding grain and our incisors for cutting vegetables. Healthy, plant-based protein sources are numerous, especially **pulses** and **legumes**. Studies show that vegetarians tend to be thinner and longer-lived than people who eat meat. There is also a lower risk of getting diseases that are linked to meat-eating, such as **kidney stones**, **diabetes**, **arthritis**, **gum disease**, **obesity** and **acne**. To eat meat or not eat meat?

**IF YOU CARE ABOUT THE PLANET, PEOPLE, ANIMALS AND YOURSELF, THEN THERE'S ONLY ONE ANSWER!**

# Humans WERE DESIGNED TO eat meat

## OUR BODIES NEED MEAT!

No matter what vegetarians say, human beings are meant to eat animals and we have the **canine teeth** to prove it. Not only that: certain types of **essential B vitamins** that give us energy are only found in meat. Without vitamin B12 we can get weak and **depressed**. Red meat also contains iron that is more difficult to get from plant sources. When we crave meat and **enjoy its taste**, that is our body telling us that we need those vitamins and energy. We should not let philosophical decisions interfere with our body's **natural instincts**. Animals don't make intellectual decisions about what to eat or not eat. Just try telling a dog that it **loves broccoli!**

**Vegetarians** think we should be able to be physically satisfied from plant foods, but our bodies have evolved to get energy from meat.

## MEAT IS THE MOST POTENT FORM OF PROTEIN.

It stops us from craving energy from other sources such as plant-based carbohydrates. Only 50 years ago, people ate balanced meals of meat with vegetables. These days, more than a billion of the population are **overweight** – this is known as the **obesity epidemic** – and that's largely due to people eating too many refined foods that are high in energy, such as **corn syrup**, **white flour** and **sugar**, instead of meat.

**CLARIFY**
depressed
intellectual
potent
ethical
organic

6

ON THE **FOOD CHAIN**, EVERY **ANIMAL HAS A PREDATOR** and this is what keeps the species in **balance**. If humans were to stop eating meat, then some of the animals we eat, such as pigs and cows and chickens, would get **out of control** and have to be killed, with no benefit to anyone.

It is possible to eat meat and still be a **spiritual, ethical person. Indigenous people** around the world, who have a **profound connection** with their natural environment and the creatures in it, eat meat. They **thank the animal** it comes from before they eat. We have the choice to do this and to buy meat that is **organic** and ethically raised so that we can feel good about eating meat – in our **minds** as well as our **bodies.**

**FACT OR OPINION?**

"No matter what vegetarians say, human beings are meant to eat animals and we have the canine teeth to prove it."

What is the evidence to support this statement? Research to support your answer.

**SUMMARISE**

Arguments { **FOR** Eating Meat
**AGAINST** Eating Meat

Summarise the main ideas for each topic.

# MODELS IN ADVERTISEMENTS GIVE US A BAD BODY IMAGE

**I think** it's shocking the way **advertisements** make us **feel bad** about how we look and distract us from the real issues of importance in the world. Images of models stare out at us from nearly all of the **200** to **400** ads we see each day. They make it seem as if it's important to own the latest fashion when our dying planet needs us to **stop buying so much** and pay attention to what really counts. I'm so sick of having these images shoved into my face, I want to **vomit** them all back up.

**Bulimia** and **anorexia nervosa** are two eating disorders that are practically unknown in countries where there is no **advertising**. But, in our society, they are on the rise. Those who are affected by anorexia can be surrounded by food and be **starving to death**.

Teenagers are getting **plastic surgery** to alter their bodies before they have even finished growing.

## CLARIFY
bulimia
anorexia nervosa
plastic surgery
Renaissance times

## FACT OR OPINION?
"Teenagers are getting plastic surgery to alter their bodies before they have even finished growing."

What is the evidence to support this statement? Research to support your answer.

A British survey showed that nearly **70 percent** of people felt depressed after just two minutes of looking at glossy magazines. The pictures of the models aren't even real. I spoke with a model who said that the magazines use computer programmes to make models look thinner, "correct" **imperfect body parts** and airbrush out any pimples or freckles. She confessed that she couldn't even recognise herself in most pictures!

## ADS ARE DESIGNED TO MAKE US FEEL THAT, IF WE BUY THINGS, WE WILL LOOK MORE BEAUTIFUL AND THEREFORE BE HAPPIER.

But standards of beauty change according to time and place. In **Renaissance** times, big women were fashionable. In parts of **Africa**, men wear makeup and jewellery to attract women. In some parts of the world, people wear many neck rings to stretch their necks because that is considered beautiful.

Ideals and ideas about beauty come and go, but what stays the same is the importance of **inner beauty**. Who really wants to see ads that show models as human coat hangers with sticky-out ribcages, knobbly knees and backbones, and skinny necks?

We need to **boycott** these ads and show how stupid they are by spending our precious time, money, thoughts and feelings on **caring for ourselves**, each other and the planet.

# Models
## IN ADVERTISEMENTS
### ARE GOOD *role models*

## I THINK THERE'S A LOT OF GOOD THAT COULD BE DONE IF ONLY SOME OF OUR COUNTRY'S MOST VISIBLE FEMALE ROLE MODELS WOULD STICK THEIR NECKS OUT, AND LEAD.

Models in advertisements give us **something to aspire to**. They are willing to take risks in starting new trends, they show us a physical ideal of how we could look and live, and they show us **products** we can use to achieve that look. Models demonstrate the importance of being the best we can be. They encourage us to lose weight, look after our skin and be **healthier**.

I don't think that images of models in ads cause **eating disorders**. As a famous supermodel recently said, "Does looking at my picture make you want to spew?" Let's face it, who really wants to see boring, ordinary-looking or ageing people telling us how to live? Models in ads show us **how great life can be** when we invest in ourselves and care about our beauty and attractiveness.

**FACTS OR OPINION?**

"Models... show us a physical ideal of how we could look and live."

"Models... show us products we can use to achieve [their] look."

What do you think? Why?

It's important to have ads so that we can **know what to buy** and where to find it. If there were no ads, people wouldn't be able to sell things and our whole economy would collapse.

Advertisements are necessary to stop our economy and the material standards of our society from **going backwards**.

Society couldn't function without ads. No one would know **where to buy things** or what was on offer. Everyone has to **advertise**, including charities and organisations that contribute to good causes – and why shouldn't they use **attractive models** who **catch the eye** to do that?

It's ridiculous to claim that people shouldn't care about **beauty** and **the way people look**. Robert Buckingham, the director of Melbourne Fashion Week, says, "There's nothing sadder than people who **don't take care** with their appearance." **MODELS IN ADVERTISEMENTS PROVIDE US WITH STANDARDS.**

Since the beginning of time, people have been **beautifying** and **adorning** themselves.

In advertisements, human beauty is **celebrated** and there's nothing wrong with **that!**

**FACT OR OPINION?**
"There's nothing sadder than people who don't take care with their appearance."
What do you think? Why?

**PERSUASIVE LANGUAGE**
How has the author used the power of words to manipulate your feelings? What words have positive associations for you? Why?

# WAGE WAR ON GLOBAL WARMING

**EMOTIONAL APPEAL**

How has the author used emotional appeal to influence the reader to Reduce, Reuse and Recycle?

**Human beings** created global warming and human beings need to **fix it**. The world is getting hotter. **Extreme weather** events such as cyclones, tornadoes, tsunamis, violent storms and heat waves will get worse and worse unless we **do something**. This is a critical time for the human species and we cannot rely on scientists to find solutions. They have already failed us by developing the machines, power sources and chemical processes that got us into this **mess. INSTEAD, ORDINARY CONSUMERS HAVE TO COOPERATE. WE SHOULD TAKE INDIVIDUAL RESPONSIBILITY AND WORK TOGETHER IN THIS CRISIS.**

**CLARIFY**

global warming

perish

**PERSUASIVE LANGUAGE**

Wage War on Global Warming

How has the author used the power of these words to manipulate your opinion? What happens if you change the words Wage War to:

face the challenge of

take action on

fix up

initiate action on

What words have positive impact or negative associations for you?

AN **AVERAGE AMERICAN FAMILY** USES MORE POWER THAN AN ENTIRE **AFRICAN VILLAGE.**

If we don't all **do our personal bit**, and if we keep carrying on **wasting energy** and resources, the human race will **perish**. In years to come, future generations will be astonished and appalled by our current level of consumption. It is time for us to use less energy. As the slogan says, we need to **Reduce**, **Reuse** and **Recycle**.

We can be **personally responsible** for helping to beat global warming by **walking** or **cycling** rather than always taking a car. Not only will it create less pollution, it will make us fitter. We can recycle rubbish and even become **"compacters"** – those who try not to buy anything new. We can eat less food from packets and take our own containers to **bulk food** stores. We can install **rain tanks**, use **solar power** and buy food **grown locally** and/or sustainably. **WE MUST EACH CONSUME LESS AND** MAKE AN EFFORT TO **REDUCE POLLUTION.**

Then, with luck, there will be **future generations** to tell the story of how their ancestors **fought the war on global warming** and won.

**QUESTION**

How do you think the use of statistics enhances this argument?

Research their credibility:
– Who put the statistics together?
– How and when were the statistics gathered?

**ANALYSE**

Analyse the information supporting the need for individuals to take action to reduce or prevent global warming.

**Wage War on Global Warming**

Supporting arguments **?**

Interesting information **?**

# GLOBAL WARMING:
## is there **another** solution?

**I think** it is impossible to try to get people to **change** their **entire lifestyles** to **beat global warming**. People need to use their cars to get to work. And just think about all the **machines** we rely on to help **save time and labour**: washing machines, computers, refrigerators, dishwashers and so on. Even if some of us tried to reduce our energy consumption, there

**CLARIFY**
consumption
take for granted
human ingenuity
salvation

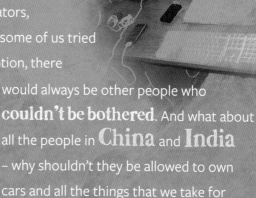

would always be other people who **couldn't be bothered**. And what about all the people in **China** and **India** – why shouldn't they be allowed to own cars and all the things that we take for granted in **Western society**?

**OPINION**
What is your stance on global warming? Why?

Recycling can use a lot of energy and it's just **not practical** to try to get everyone to put in a **rain tank** or **solar power**. Most people live in **cities** – what are people in apartment buildings supposed to do? I think we should find **new technological solutions** rather than relying on every person making changes. It's **too difficult** trying to change our lifestyles. IMAGINE **NOT BEING ABLE TO USE A COMPUTER, OR WATCH TV OR DRIVE TO SCHOOL?** NO ONE WANTS TO HAVE TO GO BACK TO THE DARK AGES.

# EVERY DAY, MORE AND MORE SCIENTIFIC ADVANCES ARE MADE.

Scientists are proposing solutions such as: **ocean pumps**, **synthetic trees**, **cloud shields** and growing **plankton forests** to absorb carbon dioxide. I believe that we shouldn't underestimate the power of human ingenuity. Years ago, people scoffed at the idea that there would ever be a machine that could fly in the sky. Only scientific solutions can bring us **salvation**. If getting rid of global warming comes down to individual choices,

## we're toast.

# NUCLEAR POWER
## IS ESSENTIAL

CLARIFY

greenhouse gases
detoxifying
radioactive waste
emissions

**Nuclear power stations** are the only way to provide **large-scale**, **cheap**, **clean** energy that won't worsen global warming. Unlike power created by burning fossil fuels, nuclear power doesn't emit **greenhouse gases**. Increasing global demand and rapid population and industrial growth in **Third World** countries demands a cheap, clean energy source. **NUCLEAR POWER STATIONS HAVE BEEN WORKING SUCCESSFULLY AROUND THE WORLD FOR DECADES.**

Nuclear power provides **France** with the **cleanest air** of any industrialised country in Europe. Not only that, it also gives its people the **cheapest electricity**. Nuclear power stations also give a country **security** by allowing it not to depend on foreign countries for other energy sources.

Some **radioactive waste** is created by nuclear power stations, but this can be **safely stored**. With rapid scientific advances, there will probably be ways of **detoxifying** it in the future. Coal-burning plants release **100 times** more radioactive waste into the environment than nuclear power stations.

The **World Health Organisation** says that, in 2004, three million people were killed by **outdoor air pollution** from vehicles and industrial emissions. Indoors, 6 million died from using **solid fuel**. In the United States alone, **fossil-fuel waste** kills **20,000 people** per year.

THE CONTINUED USE OF POLLUTING FOSSIL FUELS INSTEAD OF NUCLEAR POWER STATIONS IS IRRESPONSIBLE.

**Think about the millions** who will **die** from **hurricanes**, **floods** and **extreme weather** events caused by **global warming**. Then think about a world without pollution; a planet where every person enjoys an abundant supply of **cheap**, **clean power**. WE NEED NUCLEAR POWER NOW!

**QUESTION**

How do you think the use of statistics enhances this argument?

Research their credibility:
– Who put the statistics together?
– How and when were the statistics gathered?

**ANALYSE**

Did the argument supporting the use of nuclear power change your thoughts? Why/why not?

Points I accept and why...
Points I do not accept and why...

# END THE NUCLEAR AGE NOW

**QUESTION**

Did the debate influence/ change your opinion? Why/ why not?

**I THINK** nuclear power stations are an even more **frightening** and **dangerous** threat to the planet than global warming. **Nuclear reactors** have the capacity to ruin the Earth for all living beings. Nuclear power stations are not clean and green. They require energy to build and run and produce **deadly toxic wastes** that will continue to be dangerous for more than 10,000 years. I think it is totally irresponsible for us to make decisions now that could devastate life on this planet.

## A LARGE NUCLEAR REACTOR PRODUCES 25 TO 30 TONNES OF TOXIC WASTE EACH YEAR.

There is **no known way** of safely storing this waste. Countries do not know what to do with it. In Britain, there are **trains** that move all around the country, **never resting**, with toxic waste on board. As of 2003, nuclear power reactors in the United States have produced **49,000 metric tonnes** of deadly toxic waste. Burying this waste is not safe because containers can **corrode** and toxic waste can **seep** into the soil and water.

18

# NUCLEAR POWER STATIONS CAN HAVE MELTDOWNS SUCH AS THE ONE IN CHERNOBYL, IN THE UKRAINE, IN 1986.

Thousands of people who lived in areas where the Chernobyl reactor's radioactive waste was carried by wind have died of cancer and related diseases. There continues to be an abnormally high rate of birth defects in children born in Chernobyl.

Believing that human management of a nuclear power station will always be error-free is dicing with death. A recent Greenpeace report claimed that close to 200 nuclear meltdown near-misses have already occurred in the United States. And that's just one country; there are 450 nuclear reactors spread around the world. Nuclear reactors are also prime targets for terrorist attacks.

CLARIFY
nuclear reactor
nuclear meltdown
dicing with death
Greenpeace

OPINION
Which side, in your opinion, presented the best case – the side for nuclear power or the side against nuclear power? Why?

RESEARCH
"A recent Greenpeace report claimed that close to 200 nuclear meltdown near-misses have already occurred in the United States." What evidence can you find to support/rebut this report?

We must not build more nuclear power stations. There are many truly clean, green and totally renewable alternatives to nuclear power stations, including solar and wind power. Those are two power sources our planet provides freely, without cost.

# GENETICALLY MODIFIED food and AGRI-BUSINESS are the way of the FUTURE

**Imagine** a future world where no child ever **dies of starvation**; a world where your complete daily vitamin needs could be gained from a **single potato**. Imagine a world where even the **poorest people** could eat freely from crops that have been **genetically developed** to thrive in any environment, no matter how **harsh**.

**EMOTIONAL APPEAL**
How has the author used emotional appeal to influence the reader?

One day, with genetic modification (GM) and large-scale agri-business farming, this dream could be realised. Right now, companies are working to develop crops that will be **free from pests** and **diseases** and use less water. At the moment, growing food in small areas is labour-intensive and inefficient and the crops are vulnerable to pests, diseases and weather events.

**LARGE-SCALE FARMING OF THESE CROPS WILL PRODUCE A MUCH HIGHER YIELD AND AN ABUNDANT SUPPLY OF CHEAP FOOD, AS WELL AS UNLIMITED BIO-FUELS.**

**CLARIFY**
genetic modification
counter

The **potential** of genetically modified food is endless – plants can be modified to need **less water** in drought-stricken areas, or absorb more water in areas that flood. Genetic modification could also help to counter some of the effects of **global warming** by producing food plants that can be grown in extreme conditions. Foods will be created that will need less cooking, using **less power**. Square fruits could be packed more efficiently, creating less wastage. Fruits and vegetables that now rot within a few days could be made to last for a few **years**.

**I believe that**, with a rapidly **growing global population**, the only way to take care of our food needs effectively will be through genetic modification and large-scale farming. Food would then be available to **everyone** and, for the first time ever in human history, no person would **starve** again.

**ANALYSE**

Analyse the information about genetically modified food.

**Genetically modified food**

Evidential information **?**
(information based on fact)

Suppositional information **?**
(information based on possibility)

# SAY NO TO GENETICALLY MODIFIED FOOD AND AGRI-BUSINESS

**CLARIFY**

corporations
biodiversity
gene pool

**IMAGINE** a world where there are **extremely limited** varieties of **fruit** and **vegetables**; a world where to grow your own food would be **impossible**. Imagine a world in which diseases and illnesses are *caused* by eating fresh foods.

One day, with genetic modification (GM) and large-scale agri-business farming, this **nightmare** could become reality. THE ONLY PEOPLE WHO WILL BENEFIT FROM GENETICALLY MODIFIED CROPS AND LARGE-SCALE FARMING ARE GIANT CORPORATIONS.

**GM companies** deliberately create crops that spawn **sterile seeds** so that people are forced to **buy more seeds** (from them, of course) for each planting.

**OPINION**

What is your stance on genetically modified foods? Why?

**SUMMARISE**

Arguments
- FOR Genetically Modified Foods
- AGAINST Genetically Modified Foods

Summarise the main ideas for each topic.

**GM crops** are also dependent on **specific fertilisers** and **sprays** that are owned by – **guess who?** The same company that sells the crops! If we don't oppose genetically modified crops, one day GM companies could **control** all of the world's **food supply**. They would be in a position to dictate who could and could not eat.

LARGE-SCALE CROPPING IS **DISASTROUS** FOR THE ENVIRONMENT IN EVERY WAY.

GM crops have a **dangerous** impact on **biodiversity** and the gene pool. Already, since the introduction of GM crops into **Third World nations**, hundreds of natural **grain** and **vegetable** varieties have been **lost**. In Asia, thousands of existing varieties of **rice** have been reduced to mere hundreds.

The **massive machinery** used in large-scale farming leads to the loss of millions of tonnes of fertile **topsoil** each year, eventually creating **arid wastelands** that become unsuitable for farming. By contrast, **small-scale farming** reduces the risk of mono-crop failures and uses **human labour** rather than polluting machinery. It also encourages people to **compost**, **recycle** and **save seeds** to use again. We **need biodiversity** to ensure our **SURVIVAL.**

**PERSUASIVE LANGUAGE**

How has the author used the power of words to manipulate your opinion about giant corporations? What words have negative associations for you?

# GLOBALISATION: THE WORLD NEEDS IT!

**GLOBALISATION**, or global free trade, is creating a world where barriers and boundaries between nations are being torn down, **uniting humans** for the first time in history. Globalisation gives us **new opportunities** and chances. We can now buy a range of things, many of which are cheaper than they were 10 years ago.

The fast rate of development of globalisation leads to the creation of **better products** and **technologies** that we have rapidly become dependent on, such as mobile phones, **iPods**, computers and entertainment systems. **GLOBALISATION ALSO INCREASES WEALTH FOR ALL OF US.**

Allowing countries to concentrate on manufacturing or producing what they are best at **strengthens** and **enriches** their **economies**. The countries that are getting poorer are those that are closed to globalisation and world trade. Since China opened to world trade in 1980, its income per person has increased more than **three times** and is still growing.

**ANALYSE**

Analyse the information about the benefits of globilisation.

### The Benefits of Globalisation

Evidential information **?**
(information based on fact)

Suppositional information **?**
(information based on possibility)

Globalisation not only gives us richer economies, it creates **one world**. It makes countries cooperate with each other. Globalisation **connects all races** and cultures and teaches us not to be prejudiced and afraid of differences. It brings us closer to people from other cultures and countries by allowing us to eat their **foods**, listen to their **music**, watch their **films**, read their **books** and buy and enjoy their **clothes**, **furniture** and **design**.

**RESEARCH**

"Globalisation also increases wealth for all of us."
What evidence can you find to support/rebut this statement?

**CLARIFY**
globalisation
free trade

Globalisation makes it possible to eat at a **Vietnamese** restaurant, wearing **Italian**-designed clothes made in **Thailand**, listening to **American** music while talking on your **Swedish** mobile phone made in **China** to an **African** friend about a football match in the **United Kingdom**. AND THAT ALL MAKES YOU PART OF ONE UNITED GROUP — THE HUMAN RACE.

# GLOBALISATION IS A THREAT TO THIRD WORLD COUNTRIES

**GLOBALISATION** looks good until you scratch beneath the glossy surface to a **rotten core**. Hundreds of millions of the world's poorest people are treated as **"live meat"** to feed the forces of globalisation. First World countries use these people as **cheap labour** to produce goods for their own citizens. Men, women and children are forced into **slave-like** conditions. They work in soul-destroying, dangerous environments all day, every day, simply to afford to **eat**.

In textile factories in **Honduras**, girls and women are forced to have contraceptive injections every three months.

In **Mexico**, campesinos who once grew their own food are now forced to work in sweatshops and buy food from First World agri-business corporations at higher prices than they can afford.

In **India**, American-imported rice is no longer subsidised for the very poor.

In **Kenya**, farmland that is needed to grow food is used to cultivate flowers for export to rich nations.

**Literary Tool**
**Analogy** – a comparison in which one thing is said to be like another.
Find any?

## GLOBALISATION RESULTS IN PEOPLE STARVING.

**ANOTHER** negative effect of globalisation is that countries are **losing skills**. In the event of war or natural disaster, this could be catastrophic. If we forget how to grow food because we can import from a country that does it more cheaply, we're **doomed**.

**EMOTIVE LANGUAGE**
How has the author used the power of words to manipulate your opinion about the bad effects of globalisation? What examples of emotive language can you find?

# GLOBALISATION ROBS COUNTRIES OF THEIR OWN TRADITIONS AND CULTURE.

**Big First World companies** operating in poorer countries have no respect for **local cultures**. As a consequence of this, and the use of the English language for international business and trade, diverse cultural traditions and languages are **dying out**, leaving a soulless **monoculture** in their place.

The **ideals** of globalisation are far removed from the reality. It would be great to have an **internet chat** with someone in India, Honduras, Mexico, Kenya or any of the other Third World countries. Except that, for millions and millions of people, unless they're in a factory assembling its parts, a computer remains far **BEYOND THEIR REACH**.

**SUMMARISE**

Arguments [ **FOR** Globalisation
[ **AGAINST** Globalisation

Summarise the main ideas for each topic.

# THINK
## ABOUT THE TEXT

## MAKING CONNECTIONS

What connections can you make to the arguments and themes in **STAND UP!?**

believing in something

having an opinion

standing up for your rights

being open-minded

expressing your view

**TEXT TO SELF**

being manipulated

listening to another point of view

disagreeing

showing bias

## TEXT TO TEXT/MEDIA

Talk about texts/media you have read,
listened to or seen that have similar
arguments/themes and compare the
treatment of argument/theme and the
differing author styles.

## TEXT TO WORLD

Talk about situations in the
world that might connect to
elements in the text.

# PLANNING
## A PERSUASIVE ARGUMENT

**STEP 1**

Decide on an issue/argument. Think about the viewpoint you will take.

END THE NUCLEAR AGE NOW

**STEP 2**

Research information to support your viewpoint. Look for:

factual material and viewpoints from magazines, journals and newspapers to provide supporting evidence

statements from experts or people familiar to the public

personal comments and views from fresh angles

particular examples to make the point

## STEP 3

Think about ways you can persuade people to accept the main points of your argument. You can use:

persuasive language

statistics

emotional appeal and language

endorsements from experts and well-known people or institutions

**Nuclear reactors** have the capacity to ruin the Earth for all living beings. Nuclear power stations are not clean and green. They require energy to build and run and produce **deadly toxic wastes** that will continue to be dangerous for more than 10,000 years. I think it is totally irresponsible for us to make decisions now that could devastate life on this planet.

## STEP 4

Think of an argument that dismantles or rebuts the contrary viewpoint.

## STEP 5

Think of a conclusion that supports the initial statement.

We **must not** build more nuclear power stations. There are many truly clean, green and totally renewable **alternatives** to nuclear power stations, including solar and wind power. Those are two power sources our planet provides freely, **without cost**.

# WRITING
## A PERSUASIVE ARGUMENT

### Have you...

- clearly stated your topic and opinion by the end of the introductory paragraph?

- used appropriate strategies of persuasion? For example:

  o appeal to emotions, such as fear, pity, love of tradition, desire for success, desire to conform, self-interest

  o thought-provoking descriptions and persuasive language, such as the use of words with strong positive/negative associations

  o analogies to help the reader identify with the text

  o personal endorsement

- used factual and statistical information to support your argument?

- used quotes from experts or familiar people?

- used rhetorical questions?

- rebutted the opposing point of view?

- written a summarising conclusion to support your initial statement?

...DON'T FORGET TO REVISIT YOUR WRITING. DO YOU NEED TO CHANGE, ADD OR DELETE ANYTHING TO IMPROVE YOUR ARGUMENT?